Women who Love CATS too much.

Allia Zobel

Illustrations by Nicole Hollander

ADAMS PUBLISHING
Holbrook, Massachusetts

Published by Adams Media Corporation
260 Center Street, Holbrook, MA 02343

ISBN: 1-55850-541-5

Printed in Korea

J I H G F E D C B A

This book is available at quantity discounts for bulk purchases.
For information, call 1-800-872-5627.

For my parents, Alvin and Lucille; my husband, Desmond Finbarr Nolan, and Sheila, Patricia, Susan, Norma, and Carole, for their stamina in putting up with my obsession with "the puddies," as well as for the little darlings themselves, the ever-gorgeous and graceful Vanessa, and the devastatingly handsome and intelligent Winston-Stanley III ("the thoid")—along with women everywhere who are hooked on a feline.

—A.Z.

To all those women who have cut their families out of their will in order to leave their kitties well provided for.

—N.H.

For the gang at Adams Publishing, especially Ed, Donna, Rob, and Wayne.

—A.Z.

Introduction

I ADMIT IT. I am a woman who loves cats (some folks would say) too much.

It's an addiction I've had from birth, and one I've struggled with all my life. At first, folks thought it was just a phase. But it has gotten out of hand. I embarrass my family; I embarrass my friends. People talk about me behind my back. "She's putty in their paws," they snicker.

The sad fact is, it's all true. Nothing's too good for my puddies—not toys, fancy collars, new couches, voice lessons, not even French manicures. And even then I feel I haven't given them enough—that I'm depriving them somehow.

Worse still, I'm neglecting my husband. I spend so

much time with my cats, there really isn't much left for him. And when we do arrange a quiet moment together—usually in the garage, so the cats won't get jealous—I'm a nervous wreck! What if they think I've abandoned them?

As if that weren't bad enough, nearly all my friends have dumped me because of the cats. The true-blue few who remain have begged me to put denial aside and join a twelve-step program.

Okay, so I may have gone a bit overboard. And perhaps I do need to get my life back under control. The question is, is it too late to stop? Can I throw off the shackles of cat-dependency? Can I lead a normal life?

Probably not. But I can try. And this book is my first step. I've written it to remind myself—and other women who love their cats too much—that we can put the brakes on when it comes to our feline friends. We can take charge. We can be strong.

All we need is a little resolve. So starting today, I will not be a slave to those furry little balls of fluff. (Did you hear a meow?) What's more, those yellow eyes brimming with unconditional love will have no power over me. (I'm sure I heard a meow!) From this moment on, I will assert myself, be brave, and put my family, my friends, and myself first for a change.

Before I do, though, I just have to finish crocheting these cat booties, then put out supper. What are we having tonight? Fresh (never frozen) shrimp pureed with mashed salmon steaks and warm cream. I can almost hear them purring now.

Oh well. Enjoy!

—A.Z.

You know you're spoiling your cat when...

Your cat is on the Internet.

Your cat has a personal trainer.

You throw away at least
six cans of salmon before you
find one your cat likes.

YOU PASS UP the Kitty Litter that's ON SALE FOR the DESIGNER BRAND.

YOUR CAT GETS FRENCH MANICURES.

Your cat travels by limo.

You hire live-in help to play with your cat while you're at work.

You pay for caps for your cat's front teeth.

You feel it's important to get up and say "What a good kitty," when your cat brings you a dead mouse in the middle of the night.

YOU LEAVE the TV
ON ALL DAY SO
YOUR CAT DOESN'T
GET BORED.

Your cat travels to the veterinarian
in an ambulance.

You take money out of your 401-K
to get your cat a diamond collar.

Your cat has a cellular phone—
and an answering machine.

You take your cat and six of her
friends to see "Cats" for her birthday.

YOU WON'T TURN OVER DURING the NIGHT
NO MATTER HOW UNCOMFORTABLE YOU
ARE because you MIGHT Disturb the CATS.

You know your cat is ruining your love life when...

Your boyfriend takes you to a hit show, but you keep excusing yourself to call the cat-sitter.

Your cats demand to be tested to see
if *they're* allergic to your dates.

YOU CAN'T ENJOY SEX IF the
Kitty litter Needs cleaning.

DURING intimate MOMENTS YOU
RUB YOUR BOYFRIEND UNDER
the CHIN AND SAY "Nice kitty."

You can't entertain your husband's boss because you're too busy cooking for your cat.

You go ballistic if your date accidentally sits in your cat's favorite chair.

You talk to your boyfriend in the garage so your cat won't get jealous.

You ask your husband to sleep in the guest room so there'll be more room in your bed for the cats.

You don't mind when your cat demolishes the flowers your new beau gave you.

You FEEL GUILTY iF YOU HAVE A Quiet, ROMANTIC evENiNG OUT WithOUT YOUR CAT.

You know you're being taken for granted when your cat...

Walks back and forth over your face in the middle of the night without so much as a "pardon me."

Charges expensive jewelry from the shopping channel to your account.

Expects you to stand at attention
opening and closing doors for her
at her whim.

JUMPS UP ON the TABLE AND HELPS HERSELF TO FOOD ON YOUR PLATE.

BRINGS FRIENDS HOME WITHOUT CALLING AND EXPECTS YOU TO COOK.

Knows she can be as mischievous as
she wants and you'll always
forgive her.

Unravels your sweaters so she can play with the yarn.

Doesn't have the courtesy to call when she's late.

Switches programs you're watching to ones she prefers.

ASSUMES YOU'LL CLEAN UP THE MESS WHEN SHE RIPS UP A CATNIP TOY.

You know your cat is hazardous to your health when you...

Sit in the cargo hold with your cat
when you fly on airplanes.

Keep bedroom windows open
for your cats, even though it's winter
and you have the flu.

Spend hours petting your cat,
despite a bad case of
Carpal Tunnel Syndrome.

Strain your eyes because your
cat is sitting on your glasses and you
haven't the heart to move her.

Slip on the dead birds your cat
leaves on the stairs.

Develop stomach cramps
from testing your cat's food for
too much salt.

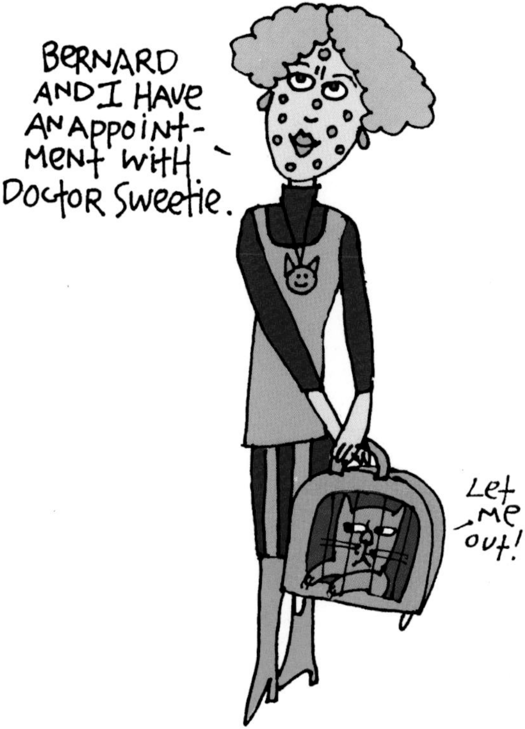

Get Hives when you have to take your cat to the vet for shots.

FEEL OBLiGED to NAP
WitH YOUR CATS DURING
the DAY — then CAN't
SLEep At NiGHt.

You know your cat is hurting your career when you...

Use a cat's paw stamp to sign interoffice memos.

Pass on a big promotion so you can spend more time with your cats.

Are asked to remove pictures of your cats from the executive dining room.

Sneak the company helicopter for trips to the vet.

ASK YOUR CLIENT IF YOU CAN HAVE SOME OF HIS BLACKENED TUNA FOR YOUR CAT.

Get complaints from co-workers with allergies about the cat hair on your suit.

Ask your secretary to buy
birthday presents for your cat on
his lunch hour.

Test positive for catnip and have
to go for counseling.

Give out T-shirts with your cat's photo as office gifts.

Are called on the carpet for making too many personal calls to your cat.

Get beeped by your cat in the middle of an important presentation.

CALL in SiCK beCAUSe YOUR CAT
WON't PLAY WiTH HiS toYS.

BRING YOUR CAT to "take our DAUGHTERS to WORK" DAY.

Add, "With love from the puddies," to business correspondence.

Keep a stuffed animal cat in your briefcase to pet during moments of extreme stress.

Don't bring work home because your cat sits on the computer and you can't bring yourself to move him.

Can't socialize with co-workers because the cats expect you to come straight home.

FEEL GUILTY FOR WEEKS AFTER
TAKING A BUSINESS TRIP.

Ruby at her Birthday
party.

PASS AROUND PHOTO ALBUMS OF
YOUR CAT AT CLIENT MEETINGS.

***You know your cat is lowering your
self-esteem when you...***

Blame yourself if your cat tries to
bury her food.

Brush and massage your cat's
scalp for hours, even though you
haven't shaved your legs for weeks.

Won't recommend your favorite novel because your cat spit up on it.

Get the cold shoulder if you spend time on yourself.

Are afraid of what your cat will think if you sleep late on weekends.

CHANGE your outfit if your cat
looks at you askance.

Worry your cat will leave you unless you buy him a new toy every time you go to the store.

Crop yourself out of photos of you and your cat.

Can't understand why such a handsome cat would want to live with you.

FEEL REJECTED WHEN YOUR CAT SITS ON the
FLOOR INSTEAD OF the PILLOWS YOU JUST FLUFFED.

tHiNK You'RE iNADEQUATE iF YOUR CAT
StAYs oUt ALL NiGHT CHAsING FLoozies.

You know your cat is making you a nervous wreck when you...

Look into cat hair transplants when you spot tiny tufts of fur on the rug.

Make a scene when your grocery runs out of "Fancy Feast."

Call 911 when your cat throws up
a hairball.

Suspect CHRONIC FATIQUE SYNDROME
WHEN YOUR CAT YAWNS.

Put baby monitors in your bedroom
to keep tabs on your cats when
they're napping.

Hire a detective to follow your cat
when she leaves the house.

Demand friends with colds wear surgical masks when they visit.

Rearrange the furniture constantly so your kitty can be more comfortable.

FiLe A MiSSiNG PerSoN'S REPORT
iF YOUR CAT iS LATe FOR DiNNER.

WAKE UP IN A PANIC AT THE SLIGHTEST
touch OF YOUR CAT's TINY PADDED PAW.

You know you love your cat too much when you...

Hire an orthopedic surgeon to clip your cat's nails.

Cancel your plans for the evening if your cat sneezes.

Blow-dry your hair in the garage because your cat doesn't like the noise.

Miss the end of your favorite movie because you don't have the heart to shoo your cat from in front of the t.v.

Go to the same vacation spot every year because your cat likes the taste of the grass.

Learn to type with one hand so the other is free to massage your cat.

CUT YOUR PHONE CALLS SHORT BECAUSE YOUR CAT NEEDS ATTENTION.

Invite your cat to "knead" your legs—
despite the pain.

LEt YourcAt Lick the SALt
OFF YOUR potAto CHips.

About the Author

ALLIA ZOBEL is also the author of *101 Reasons Why a Cat Is Better than a Man*, *The Joy of Being Single* and *Younger Men Are Better than Retin-A*. She lives in Bridgeport, Connecticut.

About the Illustrator

NICOLE HOLLANDER's nationally syndicated comic strip *Sylvia* has a devoted following from coast to coast. She is also the illustrator of *101 Reasons Why a Cat Is Better than a Man*. Ms. Hollander lives in Chicago, Illinois.